JMn

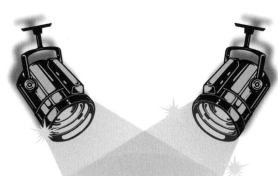

LATINOS IN THE LIMELIGHT

CHELSEA HOUSE PUBLISHERS

LATINOS
IN THE
LIMELIGHT

Sammy Sosa

Susan Korman

CHELSEA HOUSE PUBLISHERS
Philadelphia

Frontis: "Slammin'" Sammy Sosa became a baseball legend when he broke Roger Maris's single-season home run record in 1998.

CHELSEA HOUSE PUBLISHERS

Editor in Chief: Sally Cheney
Director of Production: Kim Shinners
Production Manager: Pamela Loos
Art Director: Sara Davis
Editor: Bill Conn
Production Editor: Diann Grasse

Layout by
21st Century Publishing and Communications, Inc.
http://www.21cpc.com

The Chelsea House World Wide Web address is
http://www.chelseahouse.com

First Printing

1 3 5 7 9 8 6 4 2

Library of Congress Cataloging-in-Publications Data

Korman, Susan.
    Sammy Sosa / Susan Korman
        p. cm. — (Latinos in the limelight)
    Summary: Presents the life and baseball career of Sammy Sosa, who, along with Mark McGwire, in 1998 broke the long-standing record of most home runs hit in a season.
    ISBN 0-7910-6474-3 (alk. paper)
        1. Sosa, Sammy, 1968– —Juvenile literature. 2. Baseball players—Dominican Republic—Biography—Juvenile literature. [1. Sosa, Sammy, 1968– 2. Baseball players.] I. Title. II.Series.

GV865.S59 K67 2001
796.357'092—dc21
[B]   2001042480

Contents

SAMMY AND
"THE MAN"

It was the bottom of the fourth inning and the mood was electric at Busch Stadium in St. Louis, Missouri, on September 7, 1998. As Chicago Cubs player Sammy Sosa jogged out to take his position in right field, he was aware—along with everyone else in the packed stadium—that this might be the biggest inning of the game. It might even be the biggest inning of the entire 1998 season.

Sammy's team was in St. Louis to play the Cardinals in a two-game series. Tonight's crowd wasn't just rooting for a Cardinals' win. In fact, it was early September and the Cards were already out of the pennant race. Instead the crowd was electrified because Mark McGwire—the Cardinals' famous first baseman—was about to step up to the plate again.

The previous evening McGwire had tied the major league record for most home runs in a single season. When he blasted one deep into left field, he'd pulled even with Roger Maris, who had hit 61 home runs back in 1961. Tonight everyone in Busch Stadium, along with millions of fans watching on television at home, was wondering if Mark McGwire was about

---

Sammy Sosa shows that he is truly a great competitor as he congratulates Mark McGwire on his record-breaking 62nd home run.

to shatter Maris's record with his next at-bat.

But McGwire wasn't the only one to pose a challenge to Maris's record this season. Sammy had been another hitting sensation, blasting a total of 58 home runs since April. For the past month, he and McGwire had been neck and neck in a thrilling home run race. Ironically, the Cubs were playing the Cardinals tonight. So if McGwire did break Maris's record, Sammy would be on the same field, watching.

The St. Louis crowd cheered when McGwire finally stepped up to the plate. Steve Trachsel, a right-hander, was pitching for the Cubs. McGwire waited for the right pitch, then *smack!* He drove the ball toward left field, where it just barely cleared the wall.

McGwire had done it! He'd hit his 62nd home run!

The stadium rocked with noise. Confetti rained onto the field. McGwire joyfully ran the bases, hugging his teammates as well as Cubs players.

As excitement continued whirling around McGwire, many people thought of the Cubs' right fielder. What was Sammy—the man who had been competing with McGwire all season long—doing right now?

Sammy, in fact, was beaming. Then, moments after McGwire touched home plate, Sammy ran in from right field to hug him. The two players touched their hearts and blew kisses with two fingers—a special gesture that Sammy did for his mother whenever he hit a home run. This time the gesture wasn't meant for Sammy's mother.

It was instead a sign of the deep respect and friendship that had grown between these two talented athletes.

This moving, affectionate scene between Sosa and McGwire stayed fixed in people's minds long after the season ended. Sammy then went on to break Maris's record on September 13, eventually hitting a total of 66 homers in 1998, but many fans admired him just as much for his graciousness toward McGwire.

"I've often been asked why I was so happy for Mark," Sammy would explain later, "and why I kept calling him 'the man.' For me it was just a way of showing my respect and admiration for him. Mark is a truly great player. But more important than that, Mark is a good person."

In 1998 Mark McGwire and Sammy Sosa both accomplished impressive feats within one week of each other. As individuals, they broke Roger Maris's single season home run record, and together, they reenergized the sport of baseball—and the entire country—with their incredibly close home run race.

Sammy's achievements are particularly memorable because of the many obstacles he faced along the way. He grew up in the Dominican Republic in a poor family with eight children. As a boy, he spent more time shining shoes and washing cars than playing baseball. As a young professional player, he had to adjust to life in a new country with a new language, unfamiliar customs, and intense pressure to perform. He later called his life and subsequent

In their race to break Roger Maris's home run record, Sammy Sosa and Mark McGwire developed a friendship based on respect for each other's accomplishments.

success in professional baseball, a "miracle." Perhaps that is why he has donated so much time and money to efforts to help the poor and needy in both the Dominican Republic and Chicago. He has never forgotten how far he has come since his days as a hungry shoeshine boy.

Sammy's journey from growing up in poverty to his breaking Maris's home run record on September 13, 1998, is a story about hard work, steady determination, and a strong and generous spirit. His story began in 1968 in the Dominican Republic, the Caribbean country where he was born.

2

MIKEY

The Dominican Republic is a mountainous, lush country surrounded on three sides by the sparkling blue waters of the Caribbean Sea. The sun shines nearly everyday, with temperatures usually in the 80s. Bananas, mangoes, oranges, sugar cane, and coffee and cacao beans grow in the country's rich, fertile soil. Many people vacation in the Dominican Republic, drawn to its warm climate and beautiful beaches.

Despite the island's beauty and idyllic weather, life is hard for many people born there. Poverty and unemployment are widespread, and most Dominicans live in shacks with dirt floors and thatched roofs. Fewer than two percent of the residents own a car, and there is approximately one television set for every 12 people.

Sammy's mother, Mireya Sosa, grew up in a poor family. She stopped attending school at an early age so she could go to work. Whatever money she earned went right to her parents to pay for food and clothing.

Mireya married young, and when the marriage ended in divorce, she moved to Consuelo with her son, Luis, to find work. In this small farming town 50 miles east of Santo

Sammy was born in the Dominican Republic, a country known for its warm climate and beautiful beaches. However, many Dominican families, like the Sosa family, live in poverty. Playing professional baseball is an exciting way for athletes like Sammy to support their families.

Domingo, Mireya took a job as a maid.

Soon she met Juan Bautista Montero. Juan was a strong, kind man who drove a tractor, clearing brush from Consuelo's sugarcane fields. Juan and Mireya fell in love and were married in 1963.

On November 12, 1968, the couple's fifth child was born. Samuel Peralta Sosa was a big, healthy baby. His maternal grandmother nicknamed him "Mikey," after a character she'd seen on a soap opera. Sammy's family members still call him Mikey to this day.

Sammy has many happy memories of his early years. He remembers playing with his siblings and other children and attending school. Although his family was large—two more children arrived after him—they managed to get by on what Juan earned, plus money brought in from Mireya's cooking.

In the summer of 1975, tragedy struck. Juan died of a massive cerebral hemorrhage— bleeding in the brain.

Sammy was just six when his father passed away. It was a huge loss for the young boy. Not only did he miss his loving, affectionate father, but his mother was now burdened with raising eight children on her own, with very limited sources of income.

"What I remember most about those days was working—we all worked. I started going out with my brothers, shining shoes. We would also take a bucket of water and some soap and wash whatever cars we could," Sammy wrote later in his autobiography.

Mireya also worked ceaselessly. She cooked for people and sold lottery tickets, along with doing her best to keep her family close and strong. The children shared their clothing and other possessions and earned money in honest ways. According to Sammy, she did her best to maintain a cheerful front. "[I]f my mother was ever scared or worried, she never showed it. We all depended on her and she never wavered."

The family stayed in Consuelo for the next three years. Sammy's life certainly wasn't easy for a young boy. He woke early to shine shoes. Then he went to school until the late afternoon. At night he washed cars with his brothers. Sometimes the family only had enough food to be able to eat one meal a day. Often their meals consisted of just rice and beans and fried plantains, a tropical fruit.

When Sammy had free time, which was rare, he played baseball in the park. He also fought a lot with neighborhood kids. "I loved to fight and would never back down from any challenge. I wasn't afraid of anyone," Sammy admitted later on.

In 1978, when Sammy was nine, his mother decided to move the family to Santo Domingo, the country's capital. Mireya hoped that the larger city would provide her family with more opportunities for work.

Unfortunately, the Sosas could only afford to live in a barrio where drugs and crime were rampant. They all slept together in one room. Garbage and raw sewage often filled the streets of their poor neighborhood. Many of their neighbors were too poor to buy clothing or diapers for their children.

Sammy and his brothers continued working all the time. In Santo Domingo, they washed cars, sold fruit, and shined shoes again.

Meanwhile Mireya worried that her children were unsafe in Santo Domingo because of the high crime rate. After spending only nine months in the city, she moved the family to Caciques, a country village. This move was followed by several more. Sammy remembers feeling very alone and insecure during this time. Although his mother had remarried a good-hearted man, Carlos Maria Peralta, the family's financial situation remained precarious.

In 1981 Mireya decided to move the family to San Pedro de Macorís. Sammy later called it the "best decision we ever could have made." San Pedro had many nice parks and places to play. Mireya had family and friends living there. In recent years it has become known as the home of several other great baseball players, such as George Bell and Joaquin Andujar.

Sammy was 12 years old when his family moved to San Pedro. He liked the city instantly—especially because he and his brothers quickly realized that there were more business opportunities there. They soon claimed a spot in the city's main square with their shoeshine equipment. They began shining the shoes of businessmen who worked in the sugar industry and in Zona Franca, an industrial park.

It wasn't long before the hardworking Sosa boys developed a loyal group of customers. They prided themselves on treating their clients fairly—a work ethic instilled by their scrupulously honest mother. Unlike many other shoeshine boys, they never tried to cheat customers or overcharge them.

One of the boys' most faithful customers was a successful American businessman named Bill Chase, who owned a shoe factory. The Sosa boys impressed him with their constant hard work.

One day Bill Chase's wife asked the boys to buy her some apples. When she bit into one, she didn't like the mushy texture and wanted to throw the apples away. But Sammy and his brother Jose stopped her. They asked if they could take the apples home to their mother, who was always hungry.

Their thoughtfulness—and the family's plight —deeply moved Mrs. Chase. She gave the boys the apples and urged her husband to help the family whenever he could. After that Bill Chase always brought the family gifts and clothing from his trips back to the United States.

By the time Sammy reached ninth grade, he stopped going to school. He began working full-time to help support his family.

Once in a while Sammy played sports with other kids. Because of the poverty on the island, the boys didn't own any equipment. When they boxed, they used socks for gloves. When they played baseball, they used branches or scraps of wood for bats. Baseballs were made out of cloth wound with tape, and old milk cartons served as gloves.

While Sammy joined in many pickup games of baseball, he was more interested in boxing. Like many Dominican boys, he dreamed of becoming a professional fighter. Sammy gained plenty of

Children in Sammy's hometown, San Pedro de Marcorís, watch their friends hit home runs and dream of playing in the major leagues like their Dominican baseball heroes.

experience defending himself on the streets. He began training hard everyday at a boxing school in San Pedro. He might have continued to pursue his dream of becoming a boxer if his mother had not intervened. She pleaded with him to stop and hoped that he would listen.

Sammy always tried to follow his mother's wishes. Soon he announced his new plan for the future—he was going to become a baseball player! This time Mireya gave him her blessing.

Baseball has always been enormously popular in the Dominican Republic. Children all over the country play in parks and in the streets. Every region has youth leagues and amateur league teams. Dominican fans closely follow American baseball as well as their own Dominican Winter League.

Because of his previous interest in boxing, Sammy was a relative latecomer to baseball. He was 13 years old when he received his first real glove. It was a present from his friend Bill Chase. "It was an excellent glove, the best you could find. The key is, it was blue. You might notice that today Sammy only wears blue gloves," Chase remarked later.

Sammy's brother, Luis, also encouraged him to play ball. Luis enjoyed baseball, but as Sammy's older sibling, he had too much responsibility to devote himself to the sport. He recognized early on that Sammy had a special talent and drive.

Sammy and Luis played baseball in different barrios of San Pedro. Being exposed to so many different styles of play helped Sammy learn about the sport and his own abilities. He practiced on the street everyday by hitting dried husks of maize.

Before long Sammy realized that he needed more time to develop his skills if he was going to become a professional player. By now he was working for Bill Chase in his factory. Sammy decided to ask Chase for permission to take more time off. Chase not only granted it—he hired Sammy's younger brother so that the family wouldn't lose any income.

In the meantime Luis was carefully watching Sammy train. Finally, Sammy seemed ready for the next step. Luis took him to meet Hector Peguero—a man who ran a local amateur team. Hector watched Sammy play. His initial impression was that Sammy was very strong, but was also a bit "*lobo*"—a Dominican expression for raw, or undisciplined. Nevertheless Sammy joined Hector's team in the Nelson Rodriguez League. Slowly, his game improved. He had a strong throwing arm and a quick bat. He struck out a lot, but when his bat did make contact, he hit a lot of home runs.

Sammy learned to be a versatile player from the many different styles of baseball he encountered in the barrios of San Pedro. This versatility, along with the perseverance his mother instilled in him, have been the keys to his success in baseball.

A scout, Francisco Acevedo, who worked for the Philadelphia Phillies, had his eye on the young, determined player from San Pedro. In 1984 he offered Sammy his first contract, with $2,500 as a signing bonus. Sammy was tempted to ask for more, but his mother said they should accept the terms. She said something that she has repeated many times during Sammy's life: "Be satisfied with what God gives you, and you won't go wrong."

Once again Sammy followed his mother's wishes. The contract was signed, and at the age of 15 his dream came true: He was on his way to becoming a professional baseball player.

3

LEAVING HOME

It was a happy time for Sammy and his family. He told everyone in his neighborhood the exciting news—he had been signed by the Philadelphia Phillies!

Unfortunately, the excitement soon wore off. In 1984 Sammy was working hard at Francisco Acevedo's training camp in the Dominican Republic, but he still hadn't been paid. Then he found out the reason: Acevedo was involved in a disagreement with the Phillies and the team had never received Sammy's paperwork. No wonder Sammy hadn't received his $2,500 bonus. Technically, he didn't even have a contract!

Sammy was devastated. He had no choice but to return to training with Hector Peguero in the park and hitting sticks of maize in his barrio.

Luckily, another opportunity arose for Sammy later that year. He was invited to try out for the New York Yankees. Unfortunately, the team didn't offer him a contract. Nor was he picked up when he practiced at camps for the Montreal Expos and the New York Mets.

Sammy's next chance came from the Toronto Blue Jays. He practiced at their camp in the Dominican

---

Stepping onto a baseball field for his first spring training in the United States, after many years of struggling in the barrios of the Dominican Republic, was a great reward for the challenges Sammy faced when he left his home and family.

Republic for several months during 1985, hoping to be signed to their team.

Sammy was taking the bus home from the Blue Jays' camp one weekend when two scouts for the Texas Rangers approached him. Their names were Amado Dinzey and Omar Minaya. Sammy wasn't aware of it, but Amado Dinzey had been watching him for some time. Dinzey had arranged for Minaya to visit the Dominican Republic to see Sammy play.

At this time most U.S. teams had scouts in the Dominican Republic, where there was intense competition for players. Dinzey wanted to sign up Sammy before another team did.

The other scout, Omar Minaya, met Sammy for the first time at the bus station. He was shocked by what he saw. Sammy's uniform was tattered and full of holes. His shoes were taped to stay together. He weighed only 150 pounds and looked malnourished.

Omar Minaya doubted that Sammy was truly major league material. Still the men invited him to Puerto Plata, where the Rangers had a training camp.

Sammy worked out at the camp, showing off his talents. Many of Minaya's concerns faded as he watched Sammy play. Sammy had a great arm and a powerful swing. And Minaya was very impressed by Sammy's personality.

"I always tell people that the moment Sammy got off the bus, he got off swinging. You could tell that he didn't come from much, but he had a great smile. . . . He had a great disposition and you just had to like him. He had . . . a work ethic in everything he did."

Minaya's lingering concern was about

Sammy's base-running ability. When he ran the 60-yard dash, his time was only 7.5 seconds. This was much too slow for a professional ballplayer. Minaya was still undecided about whether to sign Sammy. Amado Dinzey finally managed to convince him that Sammy's speed would improve.

The three men began negotiating and soon had a deal. When Sammy signed the contract with the Rangers, he became a legitimate professional. Best of all, the $3,500 signing bonus was a fortune to his struggling family. When Sammy received the check, he gave almost all of it to his mother. The only thing he bought for himself was a blue bicycle.

Sammy worked harder than ever before. He practiced everyday at the Olympic Center in Santo Domingo. Bill Chase gave him weights to help him build his upper body strength. Chase also advised Sammy to run on the beach everyday to strengthen his leg muscles.

In February 1986 the Rangers arranged a special practice for their Dominican players. The players' performances would determine who would be invited to the team's spring training in the United States.

Going into the practice, Sammy had his usual confidence. He impressed the scouts with his arm strength, powerful batting, and aggressive attitude. He was thrilled when he was offered a chance to go to Plant City, Florida, to train with the other Rangers prospects.

Sammy's entire family accompanied him to the airport. It was an exciting event for the Sosas—none of them had traveled on an airplane before.

Mireya Sosa was extremely proud of her son. She knew that this was the chance of a lifetime. However, she was also very sad when Sammy left for the United States. Through the plane window, he flashed her a thumbs-up signal. All she could do was cry.

Sammy was determined to make the most of the opportunity to play in the United States, however, he faced some major obstacles. For one thing, he didn't speak much English. He had to learn how to do many things for the first time—rent an apartment, shop for groceries, pay bills, and live on his own, without his family. He also had the pressure of knowing that his mother and siblings back in the Dominican Republic were dependent upon him for income. Most of his $700-a-month salary went right to his mother.

Sammy lived with several other Rangers prospects to save money. He worked hard and was amazed by everything he saw in the United States. He was especially awed by the size of the American players. They seemed huge compared to himself and his Domini-can friends.

Sammy did well in camp. As a result, the Rangers sent him to play in Sarasota, Florida, in the Gulf Coast Rookie League. Among his teammates were Kevin Brown and Juan Gonzales, two players who would later become major league stars.

Sammy continued to develop and play well. In his first minor league season, he hit .275, with 4 home runs and 28 runs batted in (RBIs). He stole 11 bases and led the league in doubles.

When the season was over, Sammy returned home. After spending time in the United States, things in the Dominican looked differ-ent. His brothers and sisters appeared very

Sammy won the hearts of his fellow players and coaches with his friendliness and positive attitude. His smile helped him overcome many of the obstacles he faced when he came to the United States, like not speaking much English and living without his family.

thin. Meanwhile Sammy had put on weight and filled out. His hair was fashionably cut, and he wore nice clothing—including a pair of red shoes with the name of a famous rap artist, "L.L. Cool J," written on them!

When the 1987 season began, Sammy was sent to a class-A team in Gastonia, North Carolina. He had a productive season, hitting .279, with 11 home runs and 59 RBIs. He and

Juan Gonzalez, a player from Puerto Rico who was Sammy's friend, were ranked as the top two Rangers prospects.

Still Sammy made plenty of mistakes. He struck out a lot—123 times—and made 17 errors in the outfield. Despite his ability to hit the ball hard and fast, he didn't have the statistics of a major-leaguer yet.

The next season, Sammy played for the Rangers' single-A team in Port Charlotte, Florida. It was the highest level of class-A ball and a very competitive league.

Sammy relished the chance to play at this level. However, his youth and lack of formal training soon worked against him. He swung at lots of bad pitches, striking out frequently. Some of his coaches felt he was undisciplined, dressing in flashy clothes and living beyond his means. Other trainers were more sensitive to the special problems facing Latin American players. In addition to having to adjust to life in a new country, the players had extra pressure from their families to perform and earn money.

Luckily, Sandy Johnson, who was director of scouting for the Rangers, understood this. The Rangers were developing many Latin players—not just Sammy. He had learned that it takes time for them to refine their skills. When Sammy finished the season with only a .229 batting average, the Rangers management stayed patient.

At home that winter Sammy played in the Dominican Winter League. He joined the team Escogido, which was a famous team in his country. Sammy had a great season, hitting .270 and being named the league's rookie of the year. He also helped his team win the

By the time he started playing for the Chicago Cubs, Sammy had spent several years in the minor leagues learning the discipline it takes to make important plays in the field.

championship and go on to the Caribbean World Series.

Coming out of winter play, Sammy felt very confident. His spirits got another boost when he heard good news from the Rangers: They wanted him to come to spring training again—but this time with the major leaguers.

LIFE IN THE BIG LEAGUES

Sammy quickly found out that spring training in the big leagues is quite different from spring training in the minor leagues. He was given first class airplane seats and hotel accommodations. He was also given a lot more money for meals.

There was another key difference. As soon as Sammy arrived at the camp, agents and lawyers swarmed him. In the United States, major league baseball players have agents. Sammy realized that he was going to need one, too. He hired Adam Katz—an agent recommended by friends.

As spring training got underway, Sammy also attracted the attention of the press. After watching him work out, a reporter from the *Dallas Morning News* wrote, "Sammy Sosa remains the best young prospect in the Rangers organization—best speed, best arm, best hitting eyes."

Sammy hoped he would be given a chance to play in the majors after spring training. But the Rangers management wanted to give him more time to develop. They sent Sammy to Tulsa, Oklahoma, to play on their double-A team. Sammy was disappointed, but he had to accept the decision and try to prove himself in Tulsa.

As Sammy found out during his first spring training with the Rangers, life in the big leagues was much different than minor league baseball. He lived in better hotels, flew in bigger planes, and ate better food. He also had to deal with the pressures of agents and lawyers.

Sammy accomplished his goal almost immediately. He started his season with a hitting streak and played well in the outfield. Then he got his lucky break.

In June 1989, Pete Incaviglia, an outfielder for the Rangers, hurt his neck. When Incaviglia was placed on the disabled list, the managers decided to bring up Sammy to replace him. Although this was unfortunate news for Incaviglia, it turned out to be the chance that Sammy needed.

As soon as he could get to a phone, he called his mother. It was late in the Dominican Republic, but he couldn't wait to tell her that he was finally going to play in the big leagues!

Sammy joined the Rangers in New York City, where they were about to start a series against the Yankees. When he walked onto the field at Yankee Stadium on June 16, 1989, he felt a thrill. He couldn't believe it—he was in the major leagues at last and playing at one of the most famous ballparks in the world!

The Rangers wound up losing both games to the Yankees, however, in each game Sammy got two hits—an impressive debut for a rookie.

Five days later, the team was playing its second game in a series against the Boston Red Sox in Fenway Park. Another player, Ruben Sierra, warned Sammy that it would be a tough game. "Roger Clemens tonight, rookie," he said. "Get ready." Roger Clemens was a legendary fast ball hurler who had already won two Cy Young Awards—baseball's top pitching award.

The first time Sammy faced Clemens, he struck out. His next at-bat came in the fifth inning. Clemens threw the ball right over the plate, and Sammy seized the opportunity. He smacked the ball into left field, right over the "Green Monster," the high left field wall at Fenway Park.

It was Sammy's first major league home run. And he'd smashed it off one of the most ferocious pitchers in the league!

Unfortunately for Sammy, his hitting streak didn't last long. He still hadn't outgrown his impatience at the plate. He swung at too many pitches, racking up strikeouts. He also made lots of errors in the field. He lasted only 25 games with the Rangers before they returned him to the minors. This time he went to a triple-A team in Oklahoma City.

In his short time as a big league player, Sammy's batting average plummeted from over .300 to .238. He was so disappointed about being returned to the minors, he could barely concentrate. In his 10 games in Oklahoma City, he performed miserably. His batting average was only .103—just four hits.

Sammy soon began hearing talk of a trade. The Rangers wanted to win their division title. But to do that, they needed more power in their lineup. They expressed interest in Harold Baines, a player with the Chicago White Sox.

Baines was an important hitter for the White Sox and a huge favorite with the fans. However, the Sox wanted to rebuild their team by adding exciting, young talent. They finally decided that Sammy would be a good fit for their roster. A deal was struck, and the Rangers got Harold Baines in exchange for Sammy and Wilson Alvarez, a 19-year-old pitcher.

Sammy was unhappy about the trade. When Carlton Fisk, a team leader with the White Sox at the time, heard about the newly acquired players, he was unimpressed. "Who are these guys?" Fisk remarked. He'd know soon. Sammy was determined to prove himself.

The White Sox sent him first to Vancouver,

Sammy was traded to the White Sox in 1989 and was named as their starting right fielder in 1990, making him one of the youngest players in the league.

Canada, to play for their triple-A team. After 13 games he was hitting .367. Larry Himes, general manager of the White Sox, was impressed. He believed that Sammy was ready for another try at the big leagues. On August 22, 1989, the team called him up.

The White Sox were playing the Minnesota Twins at the Metrodome in Minneapolis. Sammy went right to work, attacking the ball. In his first game, he got three hits, including a two-run homer, and a stolen base. It was a sparkling performance from the rookie. The White Sox finished the game with a 10-2 win, ending the team's three-game losing streak.

Sammy stayed in the White Sox lineup for the rest of the season. He played center field, gradually winning fans in Chicago with his effort. Sammy also impressed the White Sox managers. They named him as their starting right fielder in the spring of 1990. He was just 21 years old at the time—one of the youngest players in the league.

On opening day, *The Chicago Tribune* predicted that the White Sox would finish last in their division. The team actually got off to a strong start, however, winning many of their early games.

Sammy's own performance was inconsistent. Once in a while he managed to make a great play in right field, but he also made 13 errors—more than any other player in the league. At the plate, he swung at nearly every pitch. Larry Himes, the White Sox general manager at the time, said about him, "Sammy had a strike zone then that was from the top of his hat to his shoe tops." In other words, it was quite easy for opposing pitchers to strike him out because he would swing at most pitches.

Meanwhile Sammy had problems off the field. In January 1990 he had met a woman and impulsively married her. By August the couple was divorced. His personal issues, along with the media and fan criticism of his inconsistent performance, kept Sammy distracted and unfocused. He finished the year with a low batting average— .233. He did manage 15 home runs and 70 RBIs, but he also struck out 150 times.

Sammy returned to the White Sox in 1991, hoping to redeem himself. He got off to a strong start, belting two home runs and 5 RBIs on opening day in Baltimore. But soon a slump set in. On top of that, he continually clashed with the White

Sox batting coach, who wanted him to change his swing. Then from home in the Dominican Republic came sad news: Sammy's stepfather had passed away. Sammy would later describe 1991 as a miserable season. "It was nothing but problems and heartache through that whole wretched spring and summer."

Larry Himes, the manager who'd always believed in Sammy, had been fired from the White Sox the previous season. With no one on the team there to support Sammy, the White Sox lost faith in the young rookie. They decided to demote him and send him back to Vancouver.

Sammy was crushed. He'd assumed that he'd left the minors behind for good. He played in 32 games in Vancouver. He hit .267, with 3 home runs and 19 RBIs. These weren't spectacular numbers, but the White Sox did call him back up to the majors on August 27. He finished out the season in the majors, though playing only occasionally.

Shortly after Sammy returned to the Dominican Republic that fall, he met a woman named Sonia in a nightclub. Sammy told people that meeting her was the only positive thing that happened to him in 1991. The two dated for a while, then later married.

When spring training started again in 1992, Sammy was uncertain about his future with the White Sox. He felt unwanted by the team. Rumors about another trade were in the air.

Larry Himes, the former White Sox general manager, was now working for the other team in town—the Chicago Cubs. Himes was still a big fan of Sammy, and he pushed for a trade involving him. On March 30, Sammy and a pitcher, Ken Patterson, were traded in exchange for the Cubs' outfielder George Bell.

This time Sammy was delighted to be traded. He was ready for a fresh start with a new team.

When Himes gave him the starting position in center field, he was also very grateful. He promised to play his heart out in every game.

The Cubs worked closely with their new player. They especially wanted to teach him to be more selective at the plate. Their extra efforts slowly paid off. Sammy started hitting better and also showed more focus in the outfield.

On June 12 the Cubs were playing a series against the Montreal Expos. When Sammy came up to bat, pitcher Dennis Martinez threw a pitch far inside the strike zone. When Sammy jumped back to dodge the ball, it hit his right hand and broke a bone. He was placed on the disabled list for six weeks.

On July 27, Sammy returned to the lineup. The Cubs were playing the first-place Pittsburgh Pirates, who took an early lead. On his very first at-bat, Sammy slammed a home run to tie the game. He continued hitting well, and after nine

In addition to the success Sammy has had on the baseball field, he is also a very successful family man. Here, he takes time out of a busy press conference to share a joke with his wife, Sonia, and their son, Sammy Jr.

games, his average was .385. Sammy was full of confidence—until another accident occurred.

On August 7, Wally Whitehurst was pitching for the New York Mets. In the first inning a pitch shot off Sammy's bat and slammed down into his left ankle. The freak accident broke a bone and sidelined Sammy for the rest of the season.

Sammy was disappointed about being injured again so soon after his return. But he tried to keep his focus on everything he *had* accomplished: He'd played in 67 games with a .260 average overall and had 8 home runs, 25 RBIs, and 15 stolen bases. He went home to the Dominican Republic vowing to come back healthy and do even better for his team in 1993.

Sammy had no problem meeting this goal. In fact, Larry Himes would later remark, "To me Sammy's career took off in 1993. . . . That's when I would say, 'Man, he's got it. This guy's got the stuff.'"

One of the biggest factors in Sammy's success was his confidence. The Cubs coaches had been giving him more freedom at the plate. Unlike the White Sox staff, who had tried to get him to change his style, the Cubs worked with his natural swing. Their approach paid off—by August 1993 Sammy had hit 27 home runs and stolen almost 30 bases. He was now very close to reaching baseball's 30/30 mark—30 home runs and 30 stolen bases. Only an elite group of players had ever achieved that in a single season—Hank Aaron, Willie Mays, Barry Bonds, and Bobby Bonds.

September turned out to be an important month for Sammy. On September 2 he slammed his 30th home run of the season, against the New York Mets. Thirteen days later, he stole his 30th base, becoming the first Cubs player, and the first Dominican, to reach 30/30.

It was an emotional moment for Sammy. When the game was over, he picked up the stolen second base and brought it home with him. He still keeps it in his house in Santo Domingo. For him, the stolen base symbolizes "sacrifice and faith and a new beginning." It marks his first great accomplishment as a professional player.

Sammy also bought himself a present to celebrate his success. It was a huge necklace with the numbers 30/30 inlaid with diamonds. Some people criticized Sammy for wearing such a flashy piece of jewelry. But for Sammy, it was a matter of pride. After growing up in poverty and struggling to prove himself for many years, the necklace was a symbol of how far he had come.

When Sammy returned home after the season, a huge crowd awaited him. Nearly everyone in San Pedro had turned out to say hello and congratulate him. At that moment Sammy realized something else about himself: To the people in his hometown, he was a hero.

Sammy's success in baseball, such as when he reached the 30/30 mark in 1993, provides inspiration to his many fans in the Dominican Republic. Sammy is often given a hero's welcome when he returns to his homeland between seasons.

5

A TRYING TIME

The Cubs got off to a miserable start in 1994. By early May the team had recorded 12 straight losses, which was their longest losing streak in 117 years.

Although the team was struggling, Sammy played better than ever. He began the season in right field instead of center field, and he felt more comfortable there. His hitting was exceptional. By late July his batting average was almost .300, with 24 home runs and 61 RBIs.

Sammy's success, however, wasn't exactly making him happy. With so many losses, the atmosphere inside the clubhouse was tense. Many of the players were jealous of Sammy's productivity and called him selfish. They claimed that he sometimes stole bases just to improve his own record, not to help the team.

This criticism bothered Sammy. He knew that the comments were being made because of the team's losing record. Players were looking for excuses and someone to blame. Still Sammy couldn't help feeling angry.

On August 11, 1994, the Cubs' already dismal season came to an abrupt halt. The Players' Association and the

Baseball has its ups and downs, and Sammy's career seemed to be a roller coaster ride between the 1994 and 1997 seasons. He learned the pressure of a huge salary, the boredom of the baseball strike, and the disappointment of a broken hand during a home run streak.

team owners had been trying to reach a new agreement. When there was still no agreement by August 11, the players went on strike. Talks between the two groups continued, but when no settlement came, the season was canceled.

Many baseball fans were outraged. They called the high-salaried athletes and the wealthy team owners greedy and selfish. Sammy's gold 30/30 necklace was even mentioned in the Chicago media as an example of players' excessive salaries and selfish attitudes.

The bitter labor dispute wasn't resolved until the following spring. By now Sammy and his wife, Sonia, had two young daughters, Keysha and Kenia. Being a father had given Sammy a stronger sense of responsibility. He was very pleased when the Cubs made him a new contract offer in 1995. It was a one-year agreement that would pay him more than $4 million.

Sammy was aware that this was a huge salary. He was also aware that it carried a huge price. Everyone would expect him to perform.

When the 1994 season was cut short by the strike, the Cubs finished in last place in the National League's Central Division. Because the strike wasn't settled until April of 1995, the '95 season had to be cut short, too. It was decided that the teams would play 144 games instead of 162.

Sammy immediately began proving his worth to the team. On opening day, he slammed a home run that measured 442 feet. The media referred to it as "Sammy's bomb," one of the longest home runs in recent times.

Sammy continued to play well, leading the National League in RBIs. That July he was selected to appear in the All-Star game for the first time. He considered it a big honor to be included with the best players of the game.

Sammy also wanted to help his team reach the playoffs. From mid-August into September, he seemed to carry the Cubs. Over 20 games, he had 13 home runs and knocked in 32 runs. Before long the Cubs were only two and a half games behind the first place Houston Astros. Everyone was looking to Sammy to help them win their division. The *Chicago Tribune* wrote, "As Sammy goes, so go the Cubs."

The Cubs missed winning the wild card spot in the playoffs by just four games. Sammy was disappointed, but it had still been an amazing year. "I played in all 144 games of the season, leading the league in games played," he remembers. "I was a 30/30 man for the second time. I batted .268 with 36 home runs and 119 RBIs. Twice in August I was voted National League Player of the week. . . . I won the Silver Slugger Award and was named to the *Sporting News* All-Star Team."

In the 1996 season Sammy proved his value to the Cubs once again. By early July he was leading the National League in home runs. If he continued to perform at that level, reporters speculated, he would finish the season with 50 home runs. This was something that very few players had ever achieved.

Despite his success at the plate, Sammy wasn't named to the 1996 All-Star team. Many Chicago fans were shocked when Bobby Cox, the manager for the National League team, didn't add Sammy's name to the roster. Sammy himself couldn't believe it. Once again he used the obstacle to motivate himself to work harder.

Shortly after the 1996 All-Star game, Sammy had his best week of the season. Between July

22 and July 28, he hit .400 and was again named National League Player of the Week.

By late August Sammy was poised to hit 50 home runs in a single season. But on August 20, in a game against the Florida Marlins, Sammy found himself in a tight spot. When he came up to bat, the bases were loaded. His team was looking for him to get a hit.

Mark Hutton was pitching for the Marlins. He threw a hard pitch inside the strike zone, hoping to intimidate Sammy. The ball struck Sammy on the right hand. The pitch sent Sammy to first base and brought in a run for the Cubs, but Sammy was injured. With his hand hurting badly, he had to leave the game.

Sammy intended to play the next day. But X-rays showed that a bone was broken. Sammy's season was over before he had a chance to find out if he'd make 50 homers that year.

This goal was still on everyone's mind when Sammy returned in 1997. Before the season began, a reporter asked him if he would reach 50 home runs this year.

Sammy grinned, displaying his usual self-confidence, and said, "Why not 60?"

That spring it was bitterly cold in Chicago. The Cubs got off to a cold start, too, losing their first 14 games. The managers began calling team meetings to rouse their players, and fans started bringing signs to Wrigley Stadium that read "Lift the curse." By May it was already clear that the Cubs weren't going to make the playoffs that year.

Sammy started the year slowly, too. But by the middle of May, his pace had picked up. The week of May 11-18 he hit 4 home runs, 2 triples, and 12 RBIs. For the next

month, his hitting spree continued.

But the team still performed poorly, and there was a lot of negative talk about Sammy, the team's highest paid player. He still didn't have a contract and the next year he was eligible to become a free agent. Many people thought that the Cubs should let him go and pick up some new players.

Despite the negativity, the Cubs made Sammy a contract offer on June 27. It was a four-year, $42.5 million contract that also gave Sammy a $4 million bonus. The huge salary made him baseball's third highest paid player, after only Barry Bonds and Albert Belle.

The contract started a new flurry of criticism. The Cubs' management defended their star. They argued that Sammy was one of the few "five-tool" players, which meant that he could hit for average, hit for power, run, throw, and field. They also cited Sammy's strong work ethic. Unlike some players who were making excuses, Sammy played hard everyday and never complained.

In 1996, Sammy was poised to hit 50 home runs in a single season, an accomplishment very few players achieve. Close to the end of the season this dream was cut short when Sammy's hand was broken by a wild pitch.

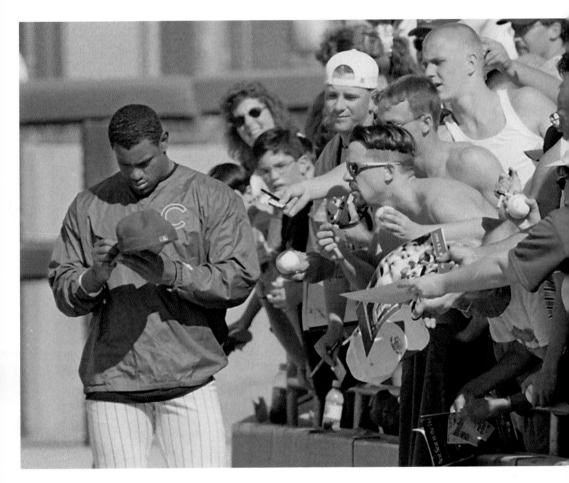

Sammy never made excuses and continued to work hard even though he and the Cubs had a few difficult seasons. This strong work ethic has made him a favorite with the fans.

Under the weight of the criticism, Sammy felt more and more pressure to deliver runs. He became more aggressive at the plate, swinging at lots of pitches. He was aggressive in his base running, too. During a game against the St. Louis Cardinals, he decided to attempt a steal even though his manager, Jim Riggleman, signaled against it. When Sammy was thrown out by the Cardinals, Riggleman furiously berated him. Sammy's teammates, along with thousands of fans, witnessed the scene.

Sammy felt angry and humiliated. He knew

his manager had a valid point, but he disliked being rebuked in front of others.

The game against the Cardinals took place on the last weekend of the season. The scene with Riggleman ended what had been a trying season for Sammy. The negativity in the clubhouse and media criticism had worn him down. He returned home to the Dominican Republic hoping to rest and prepare for the 1998 season. At that point Sammy felt he had a lot to think over. The last thing on his mind was worrying about hitting more home runs.

6

A RECORD-BREAKING SEASON

Near the end of the 1997 season, Jeff Pentland was named to the Cubs' coaching staff. As the new hitting coach, Pentland had been watching Sammy carefully. Before Sammy returned home to the Dominican Republic that October, Pentland gave him some videotapes showing other players and their swings. Pentland told Sammy to study the tapes during the off-season before the two of them started working together on batting in the spring.

The training began as soon as Sammy arrived at camp in 1998. Pentland's goal was to teach Sammy to become a more discriminating batter—to swing at fewer pitches and take more walks. Neither of them mentioned the possibility of Sammy's hitting more home runs. That was never one of their goals.

One of the things Pentland did want to teach Sammy was how to lower his arms. This reduced the tension in Sammy's arms and loosened his swing. The trainer also taught him some new footwork to help him use the power in his legs more efficiently. The two met every day, doing drills to help Sammy develop greater patience at the plate.

That spring there was sad news in Chicago. Harry Caray, a popular baseball announcer, passed away. Sammy had maintained a special friendship with Harry. He began his season by

---

With the difficulties of several bad seasons behind him, Sammy concentrated on being patient and improving his swing. In the famous home run derby during the 1998 season, both he and Mark McGwire broke Roger Maris's home run record.

dedicating his play to Harry, as well as to his beloved mother, which he always did.

Several developments in major league baseball promised to make the 1998 season unusual, right from the start. Two new teams, the Arizona Diamondbacks and the Tampa Bay Devil Rays, had been added to the leagues. This meant that the pitching talent was diluted, or spread across, more teams. In this way no one team had a strong pitching advantage so more hits might be possible.

Another development was the record of the New York Yankees. As the season got underway, they were playing nearly flawless baseball. Everyone expected this talented team to go all the way to the World Series.

Perhaps the most exciting development of the early 1998 season was the spectacular performance of Mark McGwire. McGwire was the St. Louis Cardinals first baseman. While he'd always been a power hitter, he got off to an unbelievable start in 1998, hitting home runs in his first four games and smashing a total of 11 for the month of April. If he continued to bat at this incredible pace, he was going to break the record for most home runs in a single season.

The great baseball legend, Babe Ruth, was the player who had set the record for single season home runs. In 1927 he hit 60 home runs over a span of 154 games. His achievement is especially amazing because home runs were not hit as frequently back then. The baseball used in league play was made differently and didn't travel as far as it does today.

The Babe held the record for 34 years, with no one coming close to breaking it. Then in 1961 two players launched a serious challenge. Roger Maris and Mickey Mantle, both New York Yankees, began belting out home run after home run. By September Maris had 56, and Mantle, 53. Then Mantle experienced a bad reaction to a flu shot, which made him ill. He hit only one more home run that season.

When Mantle dropped out of the home run race, all of the attention—and pressure—was focused on Roger Maris. Maris had a very different personality from Babe Ruth and Mickey Mantle, who were both outgoing men. In contrast Maris was quiet and disliked being in the spotlight. The pressure on him that season became so intense, his hair started to fall out in clumps!

As the season drew to a close, Maris matched the Babe's record of 60 home runs. Incredibly, in the final game of the year, he hit his 61st homer.

At first there was some controversy about Maris' statistics. Babe Ruth had hit 60 home runs in a 154-game season while Maris hit 61 over a longer time span, 162 games. Some people questioned whether Maris had truly broken the Babe's record. Eventually, the dispute was settled and Maris was declared the official record holder.

In 1961, Mickey Mantle and Roger Maris hit home run after home run for the Yankees in a race to beat Babe Ruth's single-season home run record. Maris eventually broke the record with 61 homers, which became the goal to beat for Mark McGwire and Sammy Sosa in 1998.

When Mark McGwire stepped into the spotlight in 1998, Maris had held the single-season home run record for 37 years. Willie Mays, Mike Schmidt, and Hank Aaron had each attempted to break it, or even match it, but without success. Some people thought the record might never be broken, but now it looked as if McGwire might be the one to do it.

Meanwhile Sammy started out slowly in 1998. In April and May he was still swinging at too many pitches, and striking out. But by June some of Pentland's training seemed to get results. By June 21, Sammy had hit 30 home runs—20 of them happened in June alone! Soon everyone was talking about him as a rival of McGwire as the new home run king.

As clips of Sammy's "slammers" began to appear on the news, he gained national attention for another reason. People noticed that Sammy did the same thing each time he hit a home run: First, he did a gleeful little hop and skip. Then he raced around the bases, instead of jogging slowly like some other hitters did. When he reached the dugout, he pounded his chest over his heart, then pressed two fingers of his right hand over his mouth, and blew kisses. This was Sammy's special sign to his mother. It signaled that she was in his thoughts and he loved her. This touching gesture to his mother quickly won him thousands of fans across the country. So did his open admiration of McGwire. "He's still the man," he said whenever reporters asked if he'd like to surpass McGwire's home run stats. "He's my idol."

Incredibly, a third player was also hitting clusters of home runs in 1998. By the end of June, Ken Griffey, Jr., the popular player on the Seattle Mariners, was tied with Sammy with 33. Mark McGwire still led the slugfest, with 37.

In July Sammy was thrilled to be named once again to the All-Star team. Unfortunately, a sore shoulder kept him on the bench for the actual game, as well as for the home run hitting contest, the day before the game. McGwire and Griffey competed in the contest, however, with Griffey winding up the winner. Sammy watched the event, cheering on both players.

The three-way race continued on the field after the All-Star break. By the third week in July, Sammy had 36 home runs, Griffey had 39, and McGwire led the pack with 43. By now the press was following the three players' every move, on and off the field. Fans constantly swarmed them, coming to ballparks early to watch the sluggers take batting practice.

Soon the nonstop media attention got to Mark McGwire. At one point he said he felt like a "caged animal" and was tired of being in the spotlight. Griffey expressed a similar feeling. He began refusing to answer questions about the home run race altogether.

But for Sammy, it was a different story. He seemed to embrace the attention, even enjoy it. When people questioned him about all the pressure he was under, he shrugged it off, saying it was only baseball. "There are people with bigger problems than me," he pointed out. "Believe me, I know."

Sammy was referring to hardships in his past. Pressure and stress were things he had experienced as a boy, when he spent his days shining shoes and selling fruit so his family could eat. He said that playing baseball and trying to topple Maris's record were fun by comparison.

As the steamy days of August arrived, Griffey's pace began to slow. McGwire and Sosa, on the other hand, stayed on a torrid pace. In a game against the San Francisco Giants on August 10, Sammy hit his 46th homer, tying McGwire for the first time. On August 19 Sammy briefly led the chase when he hit a home run in a game against the St. Louis Cardinals. The race went back and forth like that for the rest of the month; McGwire would go ahead for a few days, then Sammy would hit a few home runs and tie it up again.

In the meantime the home run derby was creating a lot of excitement for spectators. Attendance at ballparks was up for the first time in years. Many people credited McGwire and Sosa with bringing fans back to the game after the 1994 strike had driven them away.

Excitement wasn't just building in the United States. In the Dominican Republic and other Latin American countries, there was enormous pride in Sammy's accomplishments. Fans watched Sammy on television every time he came up to bat.

On September 1, McGuire and Sosa were tied again with 55 home runs apiece. With a few more

Sammy smashes his 66th home run of the season in a game against the Houston Astros. His record breaking feat was not only a proud moment for him, but also for his countrymen in the Dominican Republic.

weeks left in the season, it was now just a matter of time before one of them broke Maris's record. With his team out of the pennant race, McGwire was able to keep the focus on his hitting alone. However, the Cubs were still fighting for the division title, and Sammy was trying to concentrate on helping his team meet this goal.

"More than any home runs or accolades," he revealed later. "I wanted to reach the playoffs. . . . Other players had told me about playing in that atmosphere, and I wanted to experience it, to play for the ultimate prize in our game."

On September 7, the Cubs traveled to St. Louis to play the Cardinals. By then McGwire had 60 home runs, and Sammy had 58.

Recognizing that the record-breaking hit might come during this series, the Cardinals made special plans. Important people from major league baseball were invited to the series, including members of Roger Maris's family. Maris had died in 1985.

Before the first game, Sammy and McGwire held a joint press conference. They joked around with each other, keeping the mood light and friendly despite the pressure. At one point a reporter, referring to Sammy's habit of calling McGwire "the man," asked which one really was the man. Sammy made everyone laugh by pointing to

McGwire and saying, "He is the Man in the United States. I am the Man in the Dominican Republic."

During the first game of the series McGwire hit his 61st home run, tying Maris's record. Sammy stood in right field, applauding into his glove. The next night was when McGwire shattered the record by slamming one in the bottom of the fourth inning.

Shortly after McGwire's historic home run, batting coach Jeff Pentland approached Sammy and told him that he would "pound the ball" and get right back into the home run race.

That turned out to be a true statement. On September 11, Sammy hit number 59. The next day he hit his 60th, and on September 13, he hit two more against the Milwaukee Brewers. The 62nd, record-breaking home run came in the ninth inning with his team behind 10-8. When he reached home plate, his teammates surrounded him and the crowd cheered for almost five minutes. Sammy pounded his heart and blew kisses to his mother. The Cubs won the game 11-10. When it was over, the crowd gave Sammy a standing ovation.

Breaking Maris's record was a thrilling personal victory for Sammy. But he still remembered his opponent in the race. "Mark, you know I love you. It's been unbelievable. . . . I know you have the same feeling for me as I have for you in my heart," he said to the TV cameras.

Back in the Dominican Republic fans were watching Sammy's big moment on television. Afterward people poured into the streets of San Pedro de Macorís to celebrate their countryman's achievement.

It was an unforgettable day for Sammy. He'd broken Roger Maris's record and helped his team defeat Milwaukee. He celebrated his triumph, but then he went back to the task at hand. The season wasn't over yet, and he and the rest of the Cubs still had work to do.

7

THE MAN IN THE
DOMINICAN REPUBLIC

With two weeks left to go in the 1998 season, the Cubs were still fighting to win the Central Division title. In the midst of the battle, Sammy was deluged by the media. Journalists and television crews constantly wanted to interview him about his 62 home runs. His picture was on the cover of *Sports Illustrated* and he was featured in other magazines. He appeared on television shows and was surrounded by fans wherever he went.

The season finally ended with the Cubs tied with the San Francisco Giants for the wild card spot in the play-offs. It was decided that the teams would compete in a one-game playoff to determine the winner.

The playoff was considered part of the regular season. This meant that Sammy, who now had 66 home runs, had one more opportunity to catch up with McGwire, who had finished his season with 70 home runs.

During the playoff game, Sammy didn't hit any home runs, however. Instead he helped his team by getting two solid hits. When the Cubs won the game and clinched their division, Sammy celebrated with his teammates by dancing his "merengue" on top of the dugout.

Sammy celebrates the end of a successful season with a bottle of champagne. During the 1998 season, he broke Roger Maris's home run record, led the Cubs to spot in the playoffs, and was named the National League's Most Valuable Player.

The Cubs next faced the Atlanta Braves, who had won the Eastern Division. The Braves swept the series, and at last Sammy's remarkable season was over. He finished with 66 home runs, 158 RBIs, 134 runs scored, and 73 walks—a career high. His batting average was .308, another career high. Mark McGwire had batted more home runs, but it was Sammy who was named the National League's Most Valuable Player. The League recognized his outstanding contribution to the Cubs, a team that had performed dismally the year before.

The baseball season was over for Sammy, but a new life as a celebrity was beginning. Invitations continued to pour in. He appeared on the *Tonight Show* with Jay Leno and the *Late Show* with David Letterman. He also visited President Clinton at the White House. In the Dominican Republic, President Leonel Fernandez made him an ambassador.

Sammy was also busy with something else. Hurricane Georges had devastated the Dominican Republic in late September, killing almost 300 people and leaving thousands without homes.

When Sammy returned home that fall, his heart broke at the sheer scale of the damage. Yet thousands of people—possibly as many as 500,000—still turned out to greet him.

"Most touching of all was the sight of people in my hometown of San Pedro, cheering me amid all the rubble and downed trees and power lines," Sammy said later.

Years ago Sammy had established the Sammy Sosa Foundation to help raise money for his country. Now checks for his hurricane relief effort poured into his foundation, many of them made out for $66 as a tribute to his

66 home runs. Blankets, food, and water were collected and distributed. Everywhere Sammy went—from the United States to Japan—he spoke about the plight of his people, raising more money for repairs to the island. His foundation eventually opened the Sammy Sosa Children's Medical Center for Preventative Medicine in San Pedro to give free immunizations to children living near San Pedro.

Sammy's wildly successful 1998 season made him a celebrity. He is seen here on "The Tonight Show with Jay Leno" receiving a standing ovation for his accomplishments as a baseball player.

In response to his relief efforts and generosity, Major League Baseball gave Sammy the Roberto Clemente Man of the Year Award. Roberto Clemente was a talented outfielder from Puerto Rico who played for the Pirates. Like Sammy he organized many relief efforts. Clemente was on his way to Nicaragua, to help after an earthquake, when his plane crashed

After Hurricane Georges devastated the Dominican Republic, Sammy organized a hurricane relief effort for and spoke out about the hardships his countrymen were facing. He was presented with the Roberto Clemente Man of the Year Award for his work with the relief effort.

and he was killed. For Sammy, it was an honor to receive an award named after an athlete who'd always been his hero.

Sammy went into 1999 with many people concerned about his well-being after his busy and stressful off-season. Everyone predicted that he would never match his 1998 performance. Even Mark McGwire said that 1998 couldn't happen again. But Sammy, always supremely confident, felt differently. "Why not?" he said slyly.

Sammy got off to his usual slow start. Unfortunately, the Cubs were plagued by injuries and had a bad year. However, Sammy finished the season with 63 home runs, and he was the first player in major league history to hit 60 home runs in two consecutive years.

By 2000 much of the excitement surrounding the home run race had died down. But Sammy still had remarkable numbers. He led the league with 50 home runs.

In 1998 Sammy Sosa and Mark McGwire captivated the world with their sensational hitting. Together they rekindled interest in a sport that had steadily been losing fans. They also inspired fans with their friendly, gracious style of competing.

Throughout his extraordinary achievements, and all the media attention and celebrity that accompanied them, Sammy never forgot his humble beginnings in the Dominican Republic. His background will continue to define him, to play a role in whatever else he accomplishes in his lifetime. As he himself has said:

"Why do I go back to San Pedro Marcorís? To be with my people. That's the most beautiful thing I have. I could never envision a time when I would be separated from them, because even once you've attained things in life, you can never leave behind who you are. . . . I have all this fame now, but I will never forget where I came from."

CHRONOLOGY

1968	Samuel Sosa is born on November 12 in the Dominican Republic.

1968 Samuel Sosa is born on November 12 in the Dominican Republic.

1976 Sammy's father dies.

1981 The family moves to San Pedro de Macorís.

1985 Sammy is signed by the Texas Rangers

1986 Plays in the Gulf Coast Rookie League, where he leads the league in doubles.

1989 Makes his major league debut with the Rangers on June 16. Traded to the Chicago White Sox for Harold Baines.

1990 Plays his first full major league season

1992 Traded with pitcher Ken Patterson to the Chicago Cubs for outfielder George Bell. Injured twice during the season.

1993 First player in Cubs history to reach 30/30 mark with 33 home runs and 36 stolen bases.

1994 Players' strike declared on August 11.

1995 Hits 36 home runs, steals 34 bases, and has 119 RBIs; plays in his first All-Star Game on July 11.

1996 Hits 40 home runs and 100 RBIs before his season ends on August 20 when he is hit by a pitch that breaks his hand; becomes the third highest paid player in baseball.

1997 Hits 119 RBIs for the second time.

1998 Sets single month home run record with 20 home runs in June; breaks Roger Maris's record on September 13; named National League MVP; receives the Roberto Clemente Man of the Year Award.

1999 Finishes the season with 63 home runs. First player to hit over 60 home runs in two consecutive seasons.

2000 Leads the League with 50 home runs.

ACCOMPLISHMENTS

1994   Won Cubs' Triple Crown, with .300 average, 25 homer runs, 70 RBIs

1995   Louisville Slugger Silver Slugger Award

1998   Louisville Slugger Silver Slugger Award
Sports Illustrated Sportsman of the Year (with Mark McGwire)
The Sporting News Sportsman of the Year (with Mark McGwire)

1999   First player to hit over 60 home runs in two consecutive seasons

FURTHER READING

Christopher, Matt. *At the Plate with . . . Mark McGwire.* Boston: Little Brown and Company, 1999.

Christopher, Matt. *At the Plate with . . . Sammy Sosa.* Boston: Little Brown and Company, 1999.

Driscoll, Laura. *Sammy Sosa: He's the Man.* New York: Grosset & Dunlap, 1999.

Gutman, Bill. *Sammy Sosa.* New York: Pocket Books, 1998.

Layden, Joseph. *Home Run Heroes: Mark McGwire and Sammy Sosa.* New York: Scholastic, 1998.

Preller, James. *A Season to Remember.* New York: Simon & Schuster, 1998.

Sosa, Sammy, with Breton, Marcos. *Sosa: An Autobiography.* New York: Warner Books, 2000.

INDEX

PHOTO CREDITS:

ABOUT THE AUTHOR

SUSAN KORMAN is the author of over 20 books for children, including two other biographies published by Chelsea House, *Walter Raleigh* and *Christina Aguilera.* Formerly a children's book editor, she now works as a freelance writer. Ms. Korman lives in Bucks County, Pennsylvania, with her husband, three children, and two cats.